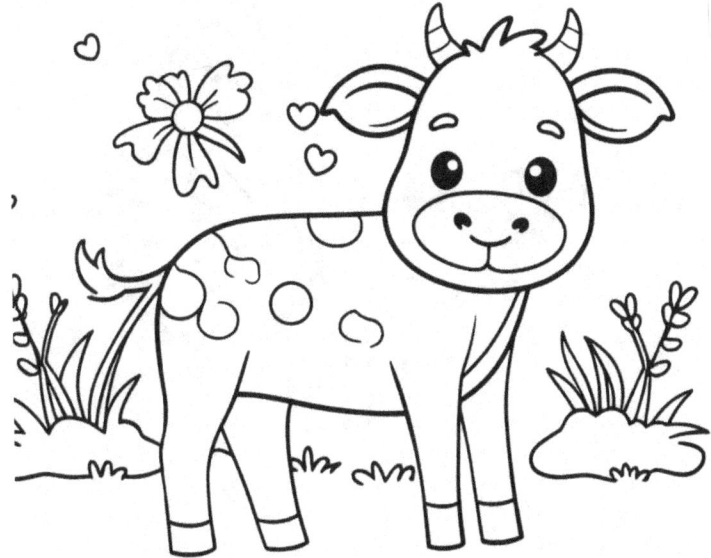

To curious minds and creative hearts,
May this coloring book bring joy and inspiration to every stroke of color. Let each page be an invitation to explore, imagine and create, transforming the simple act of coloring into a magical journey. May these pages full of life and charming animals awaken your passion for nature and art. May the joy of coloring be the purest expression of your imagination. I dedicate this book to you, the true artists, and I hope that every stroke is a celebration of love, fun, and creativity.

Claudia Costa
2024

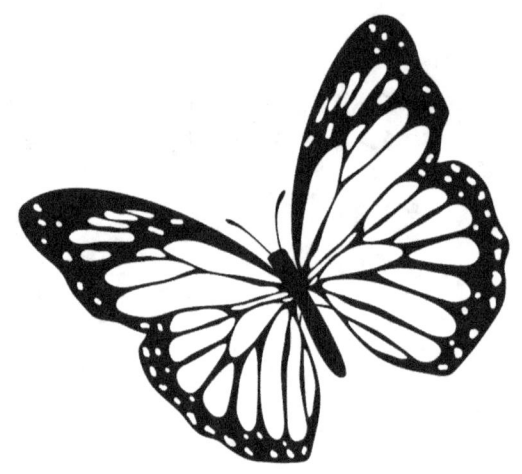

This Book Belongs to:

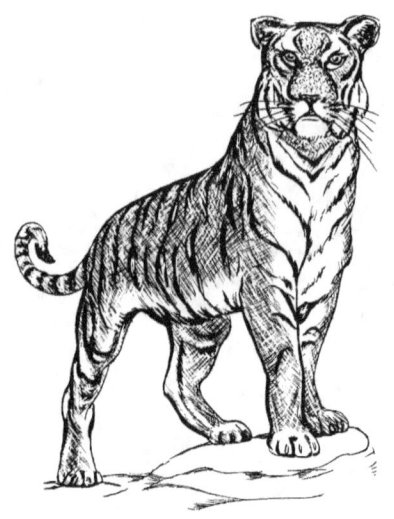

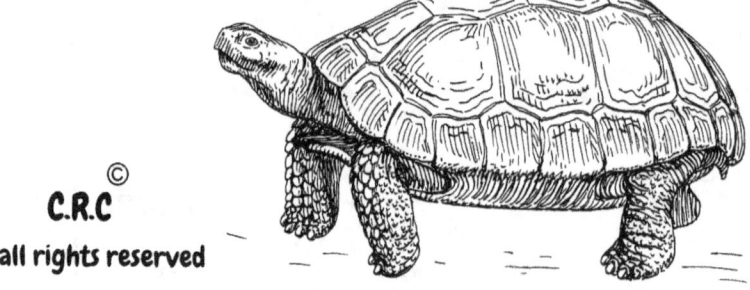

C.R.P.©
Claudia Regina publications

Test Color Page

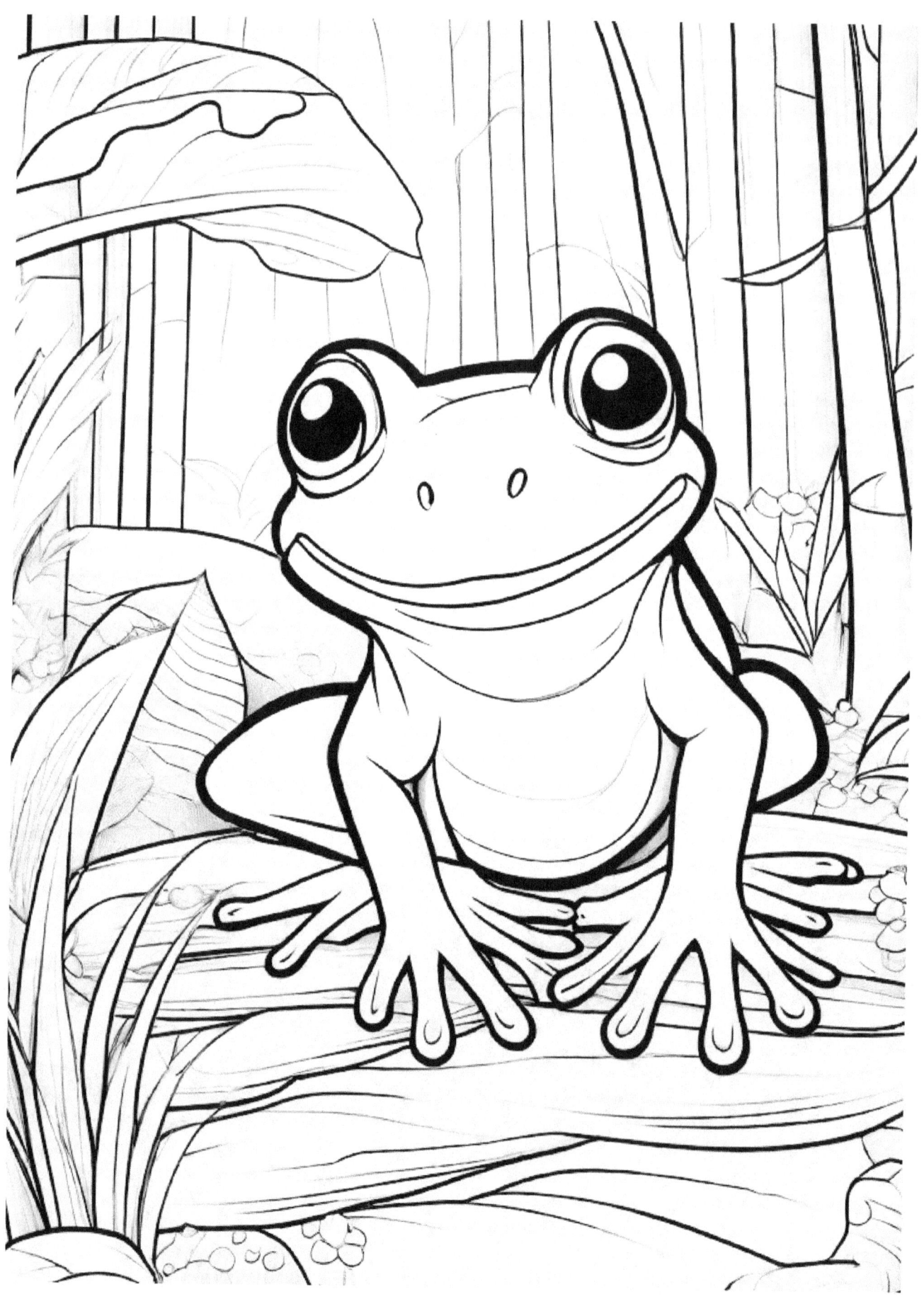

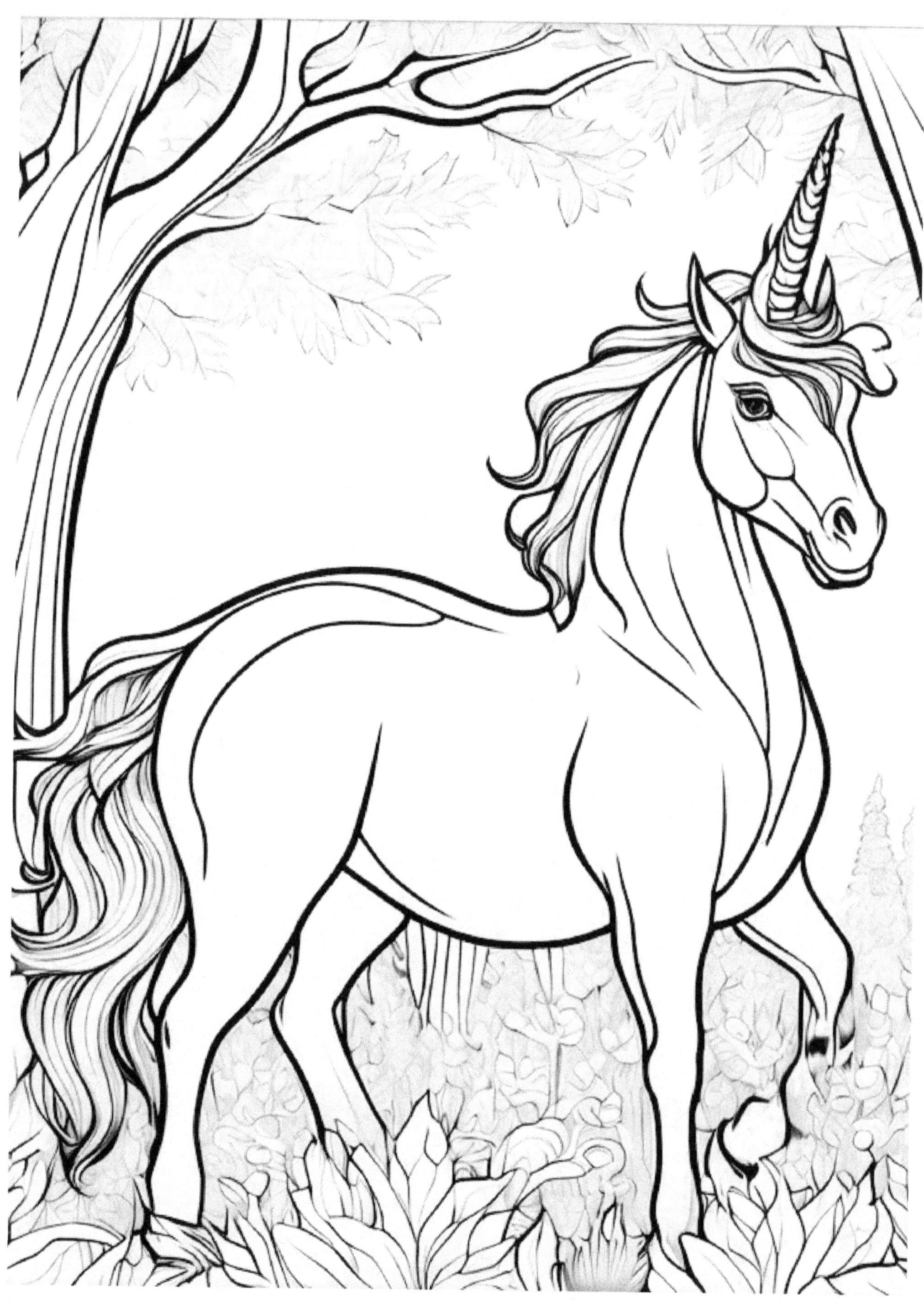

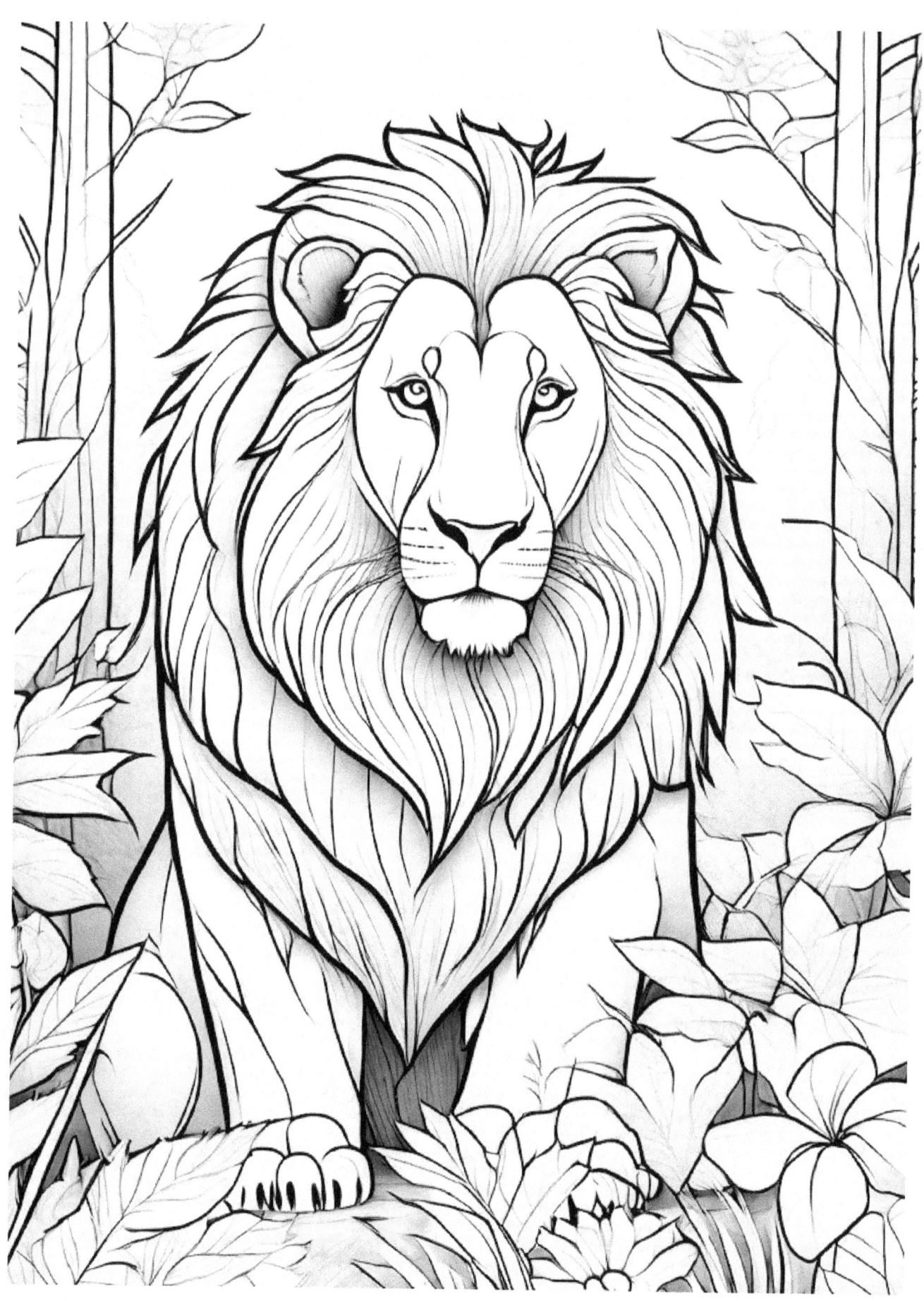

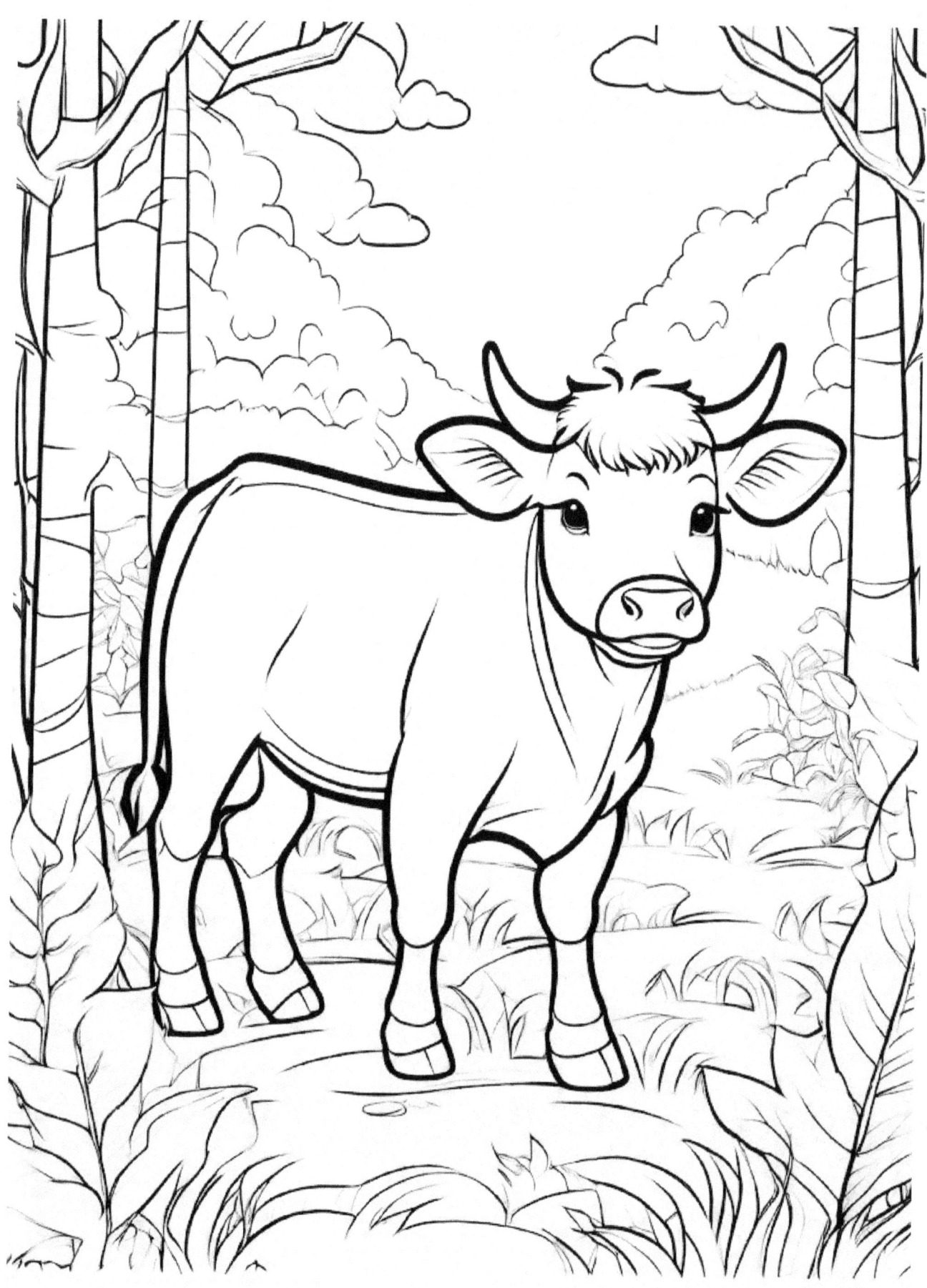

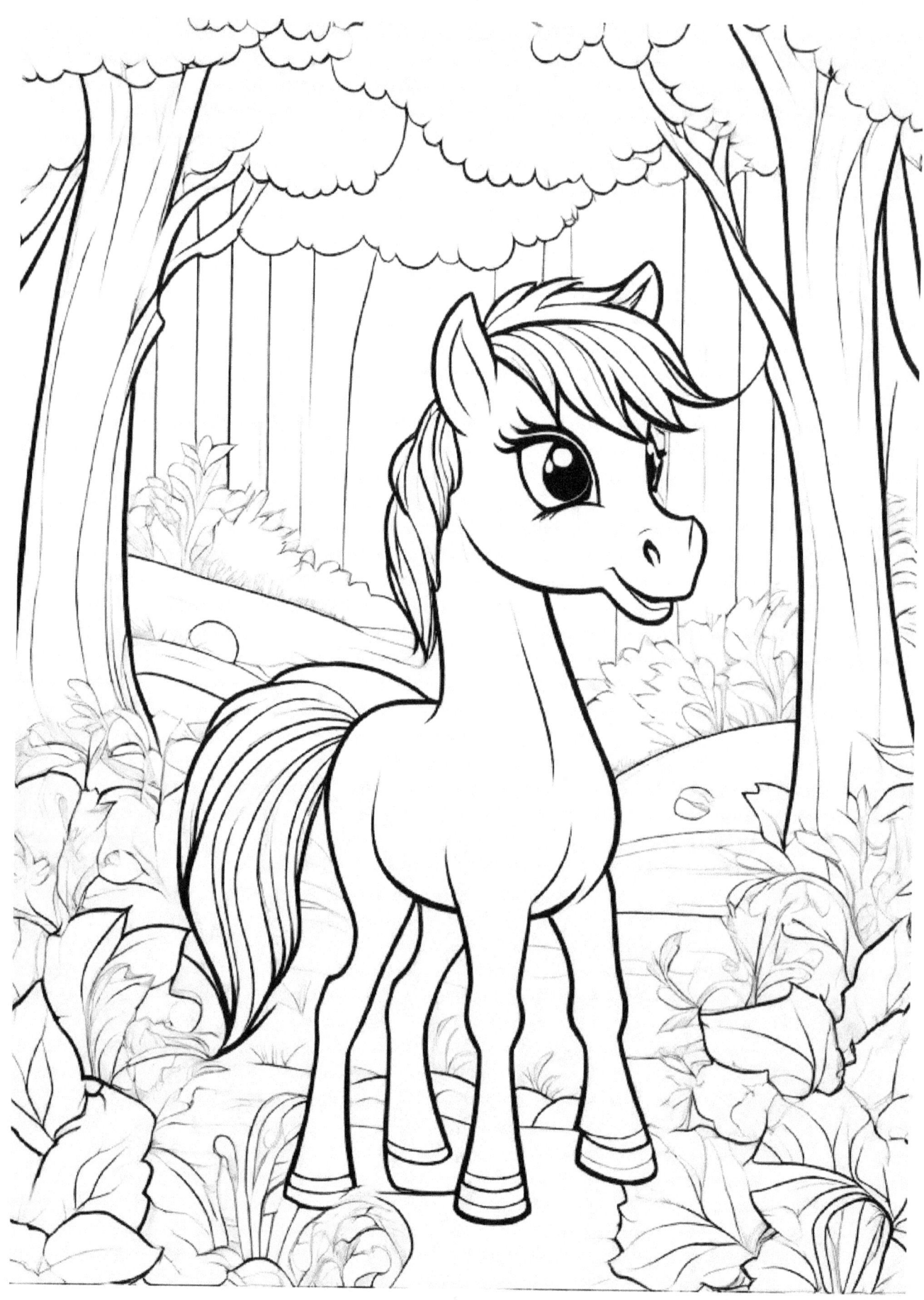

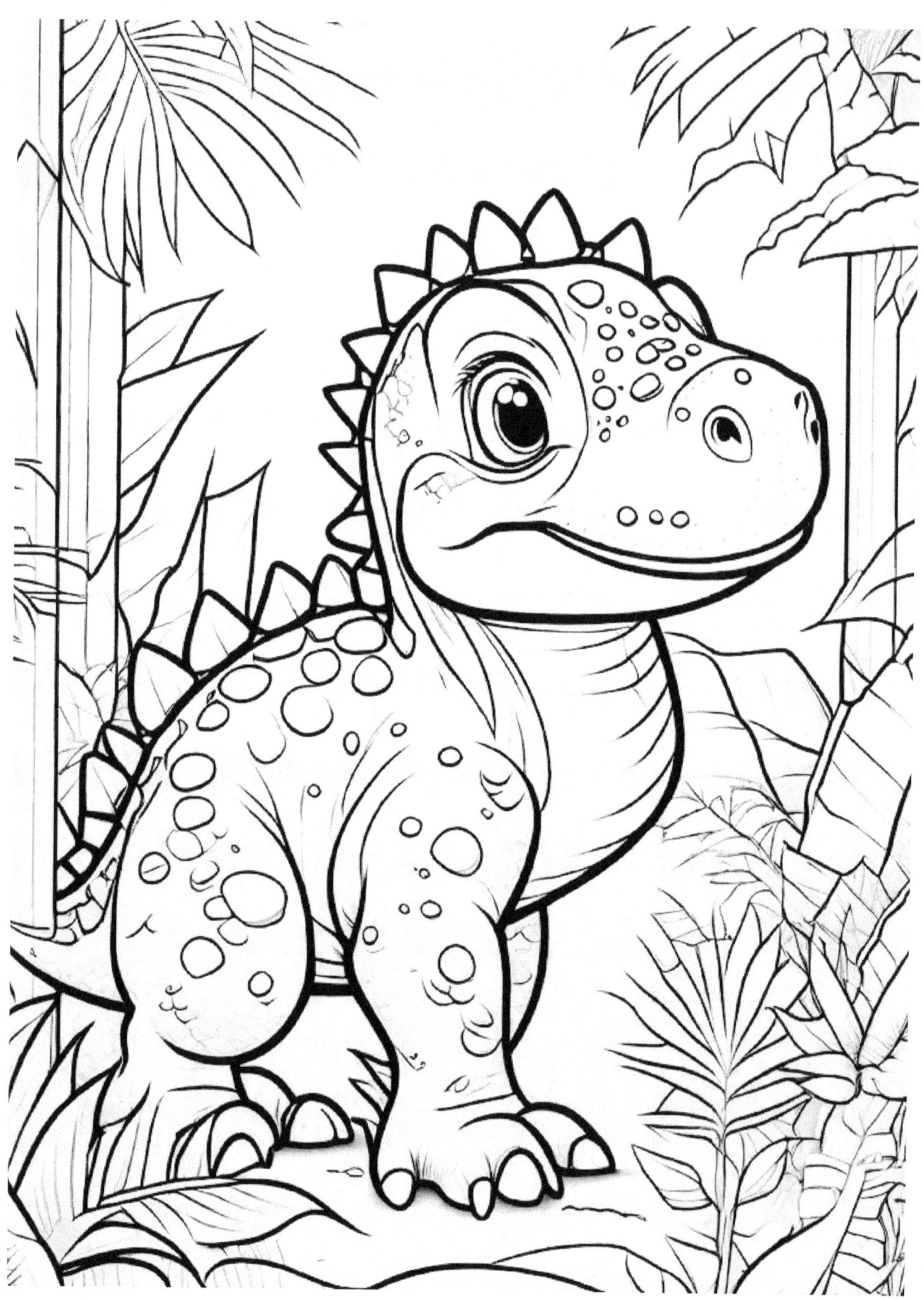

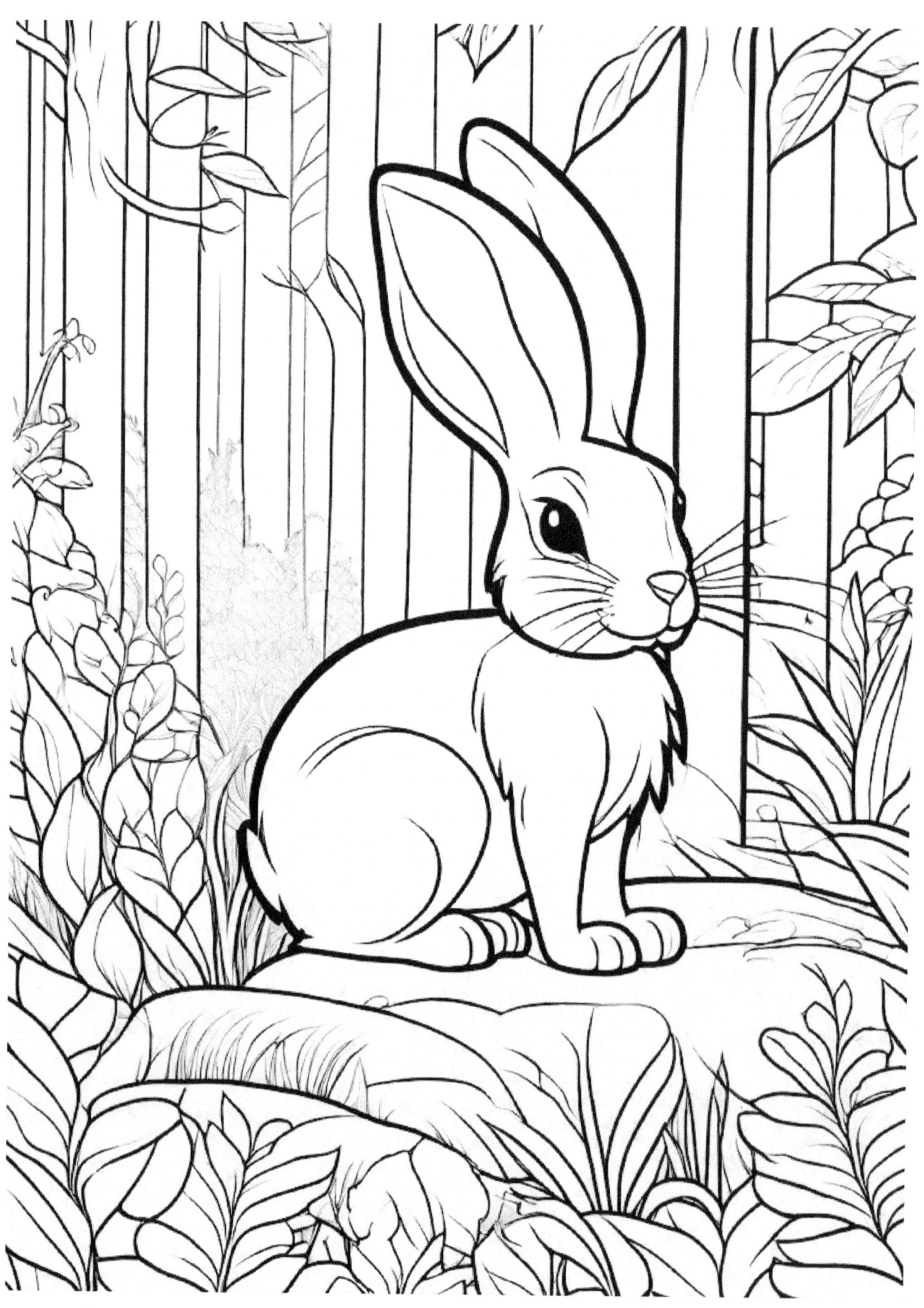

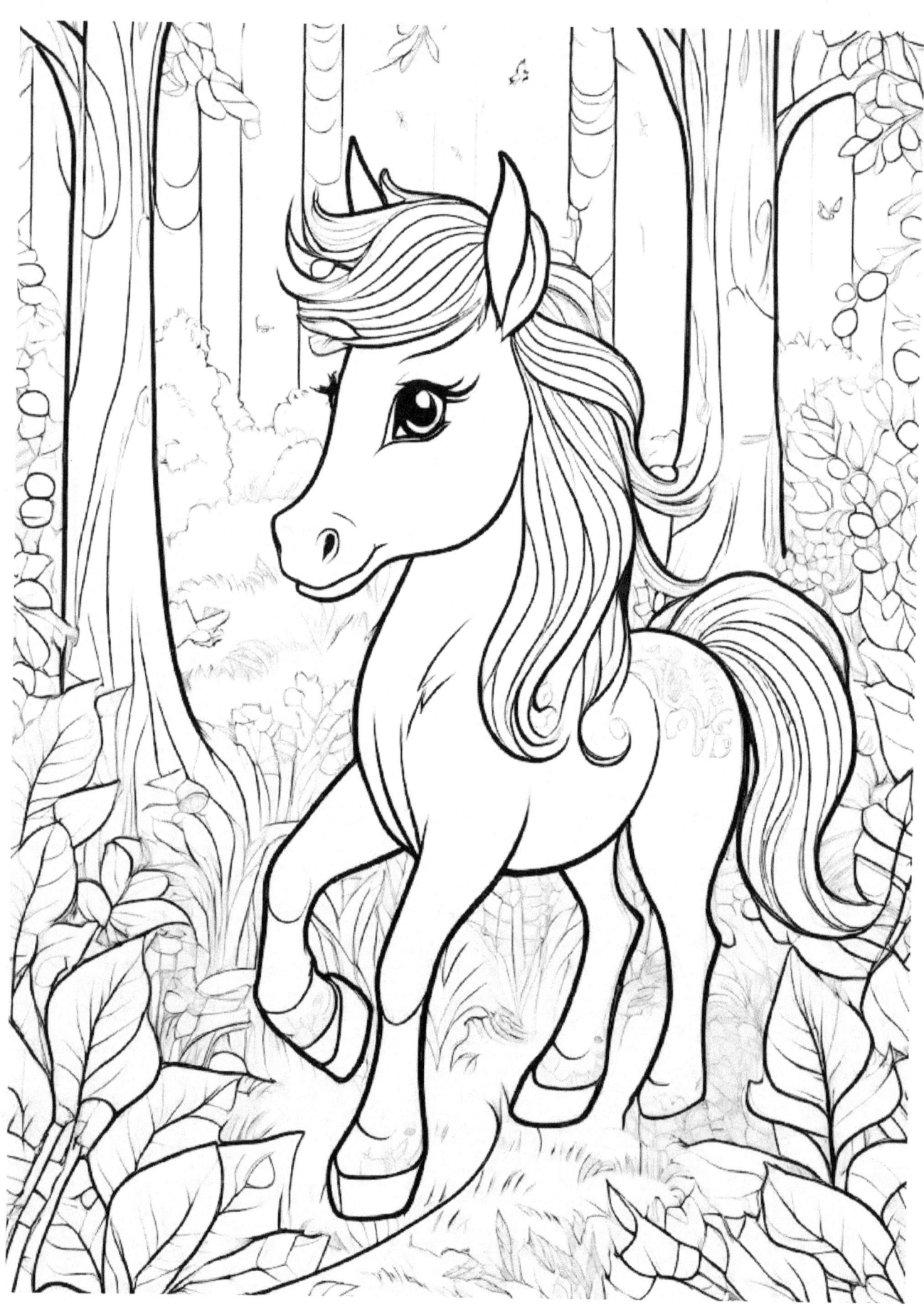

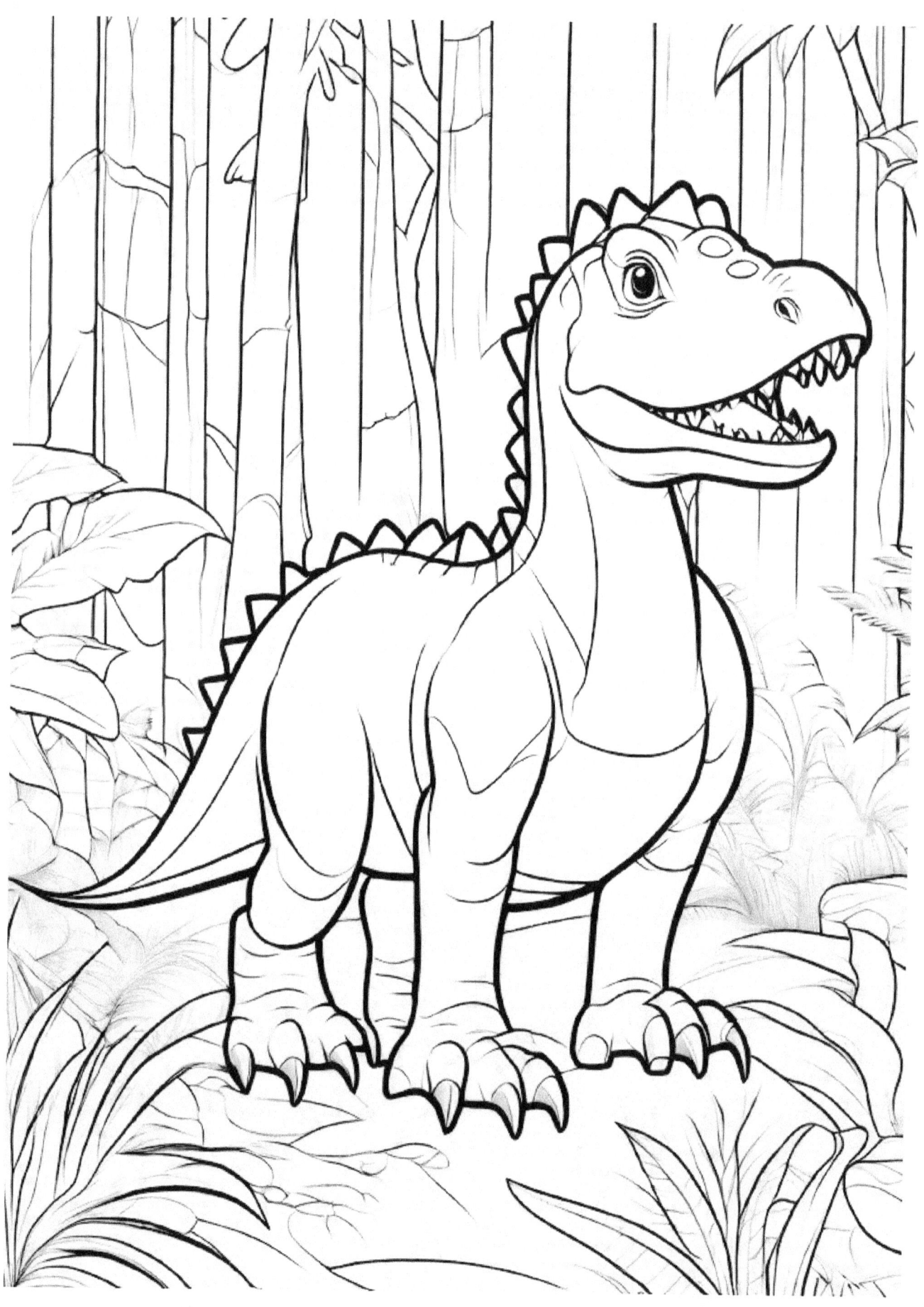

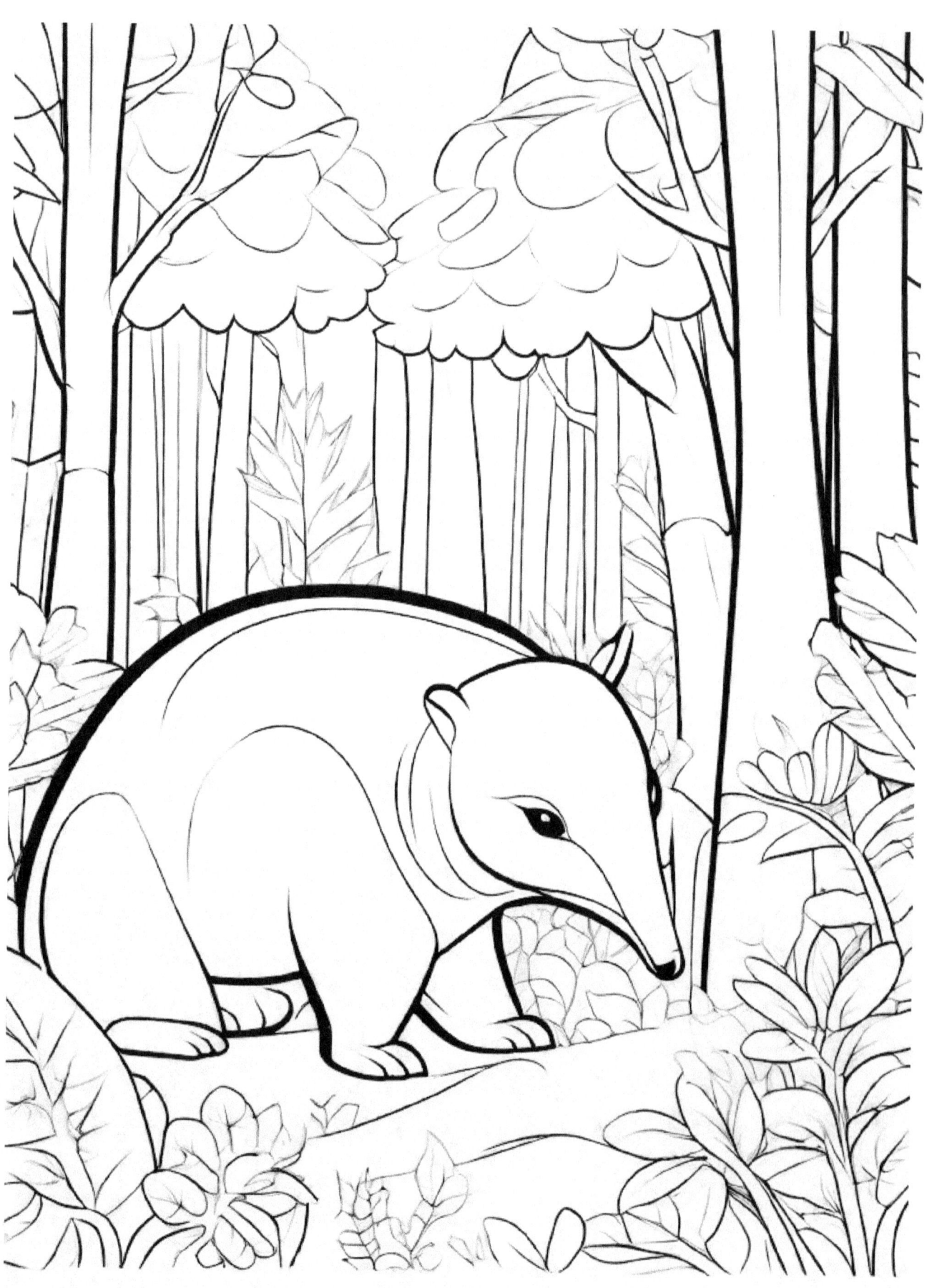

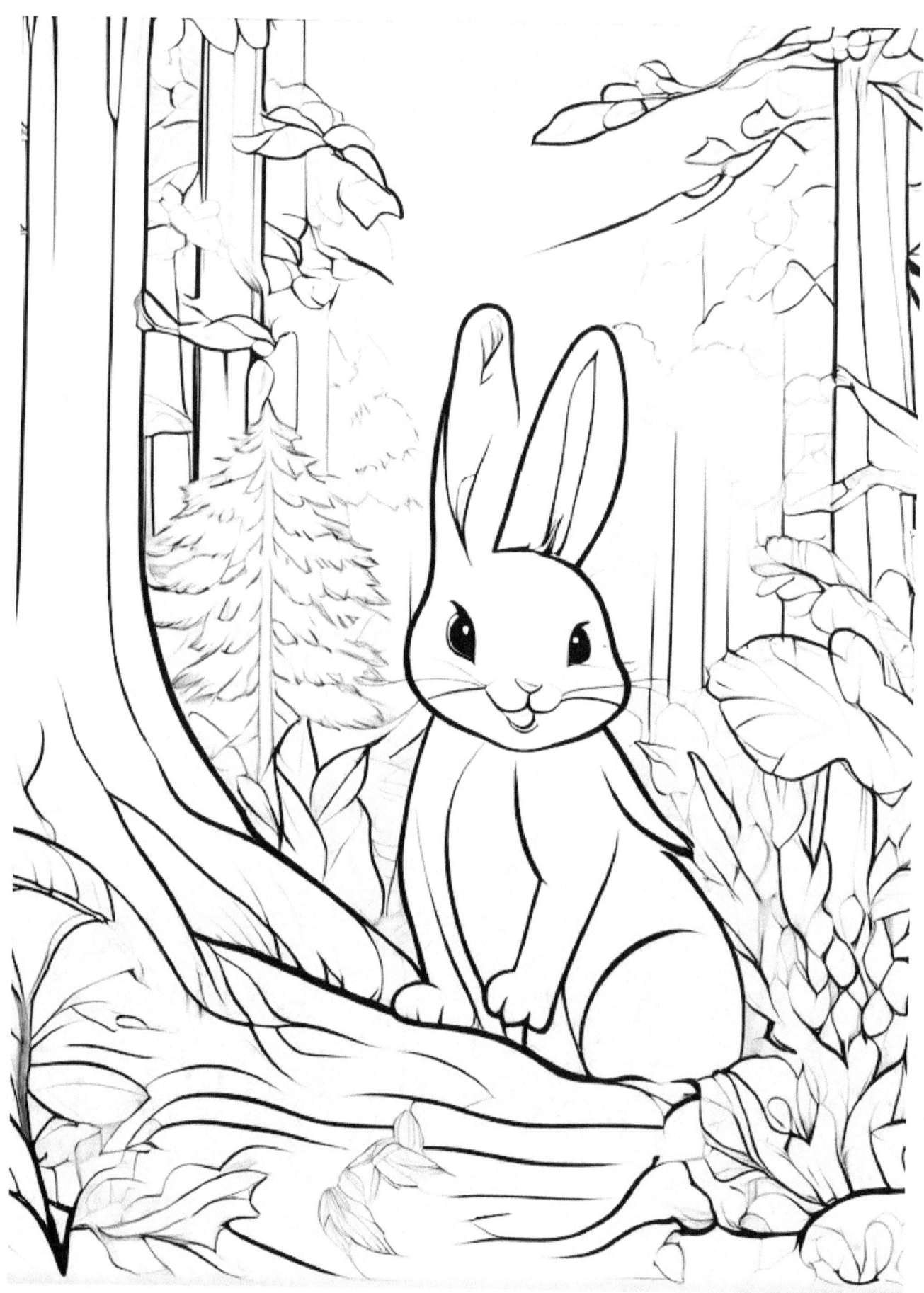

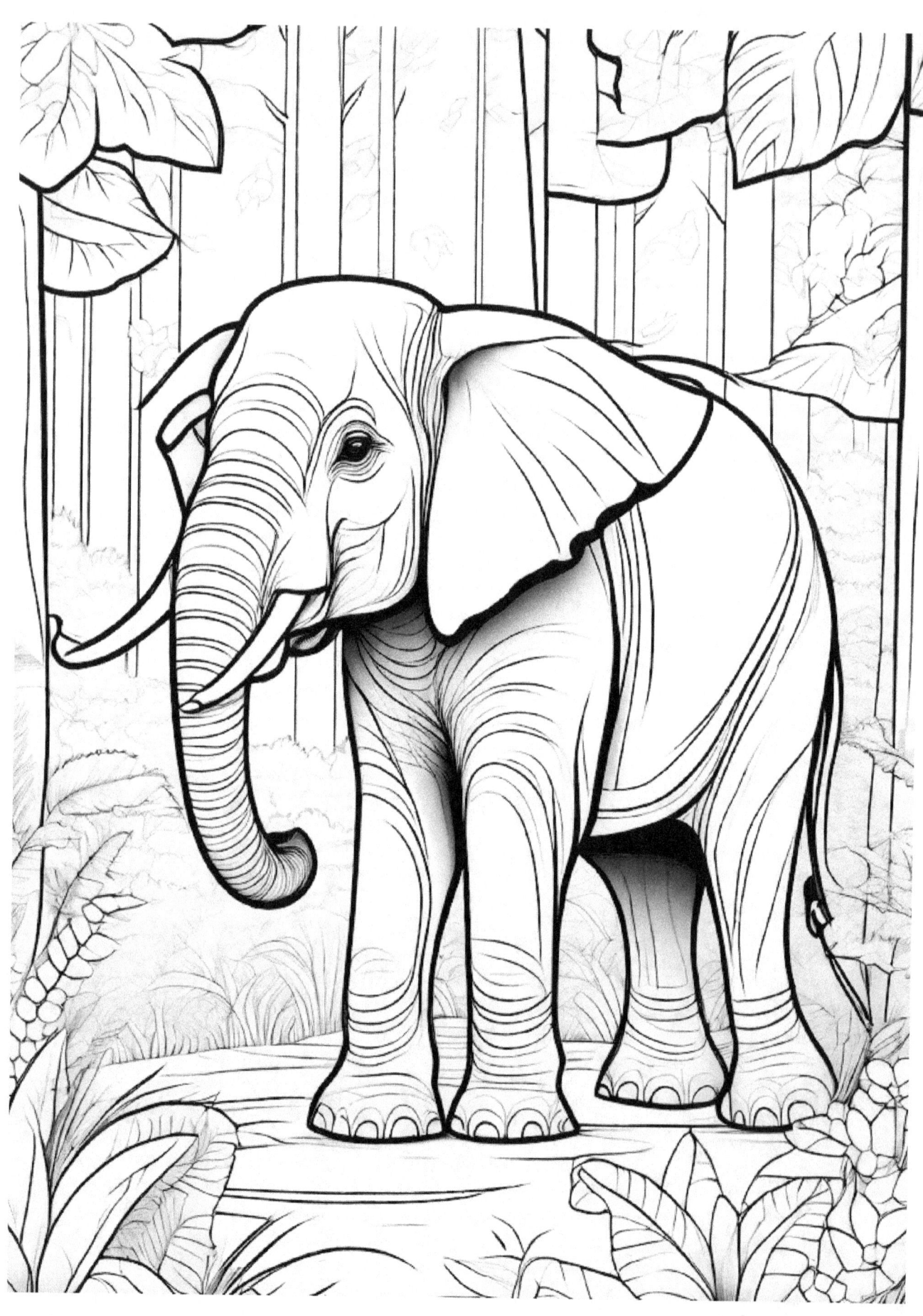

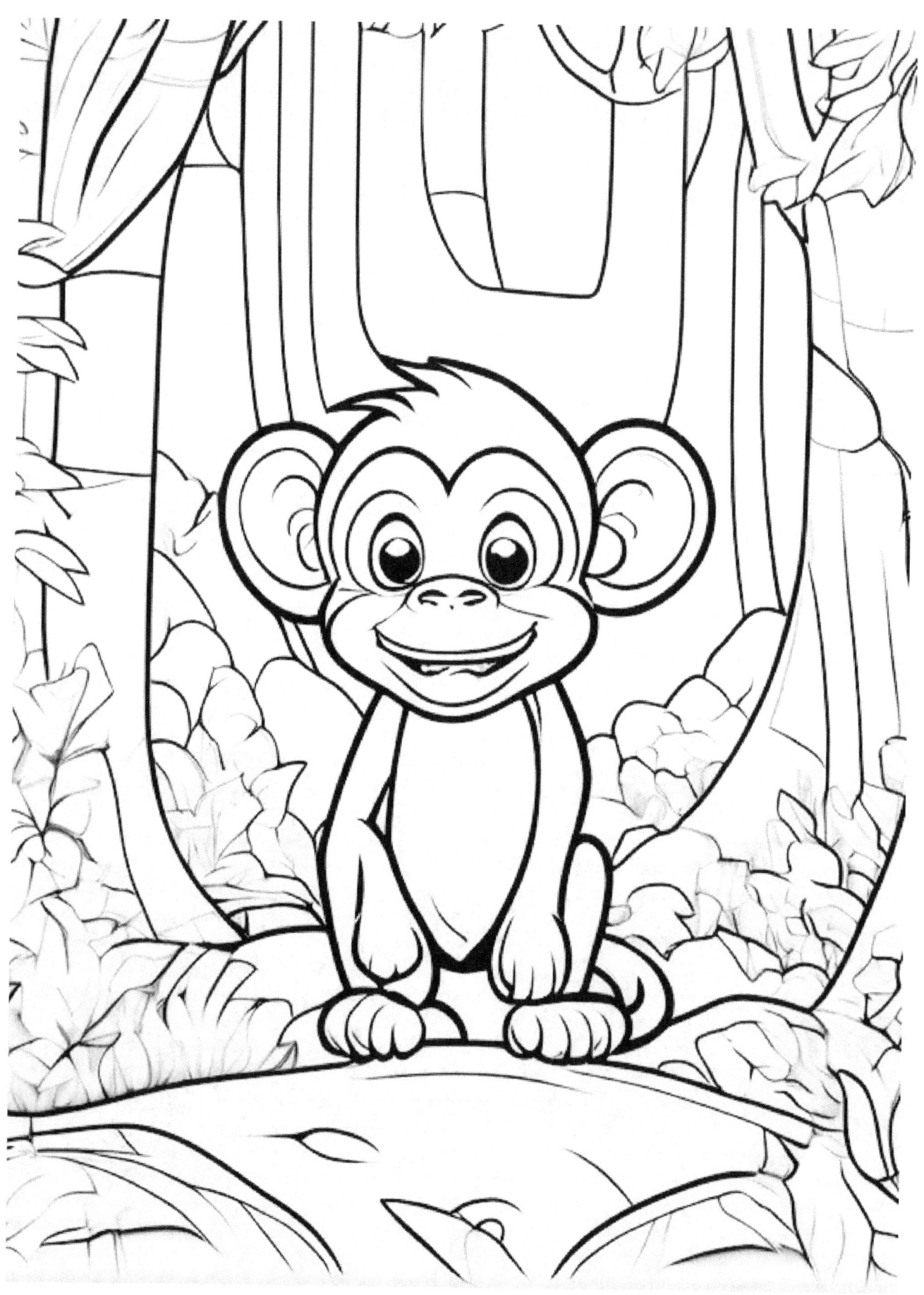

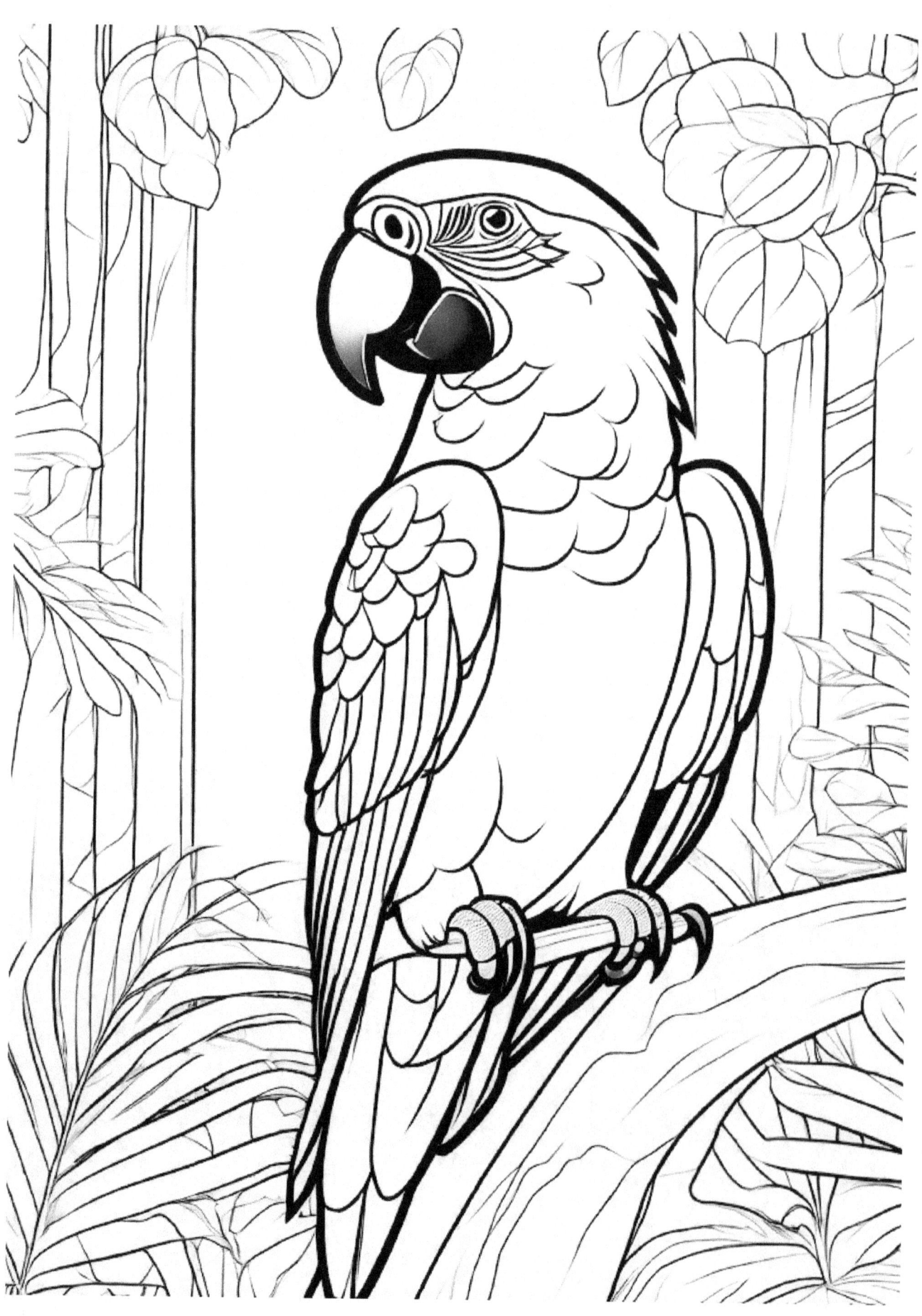

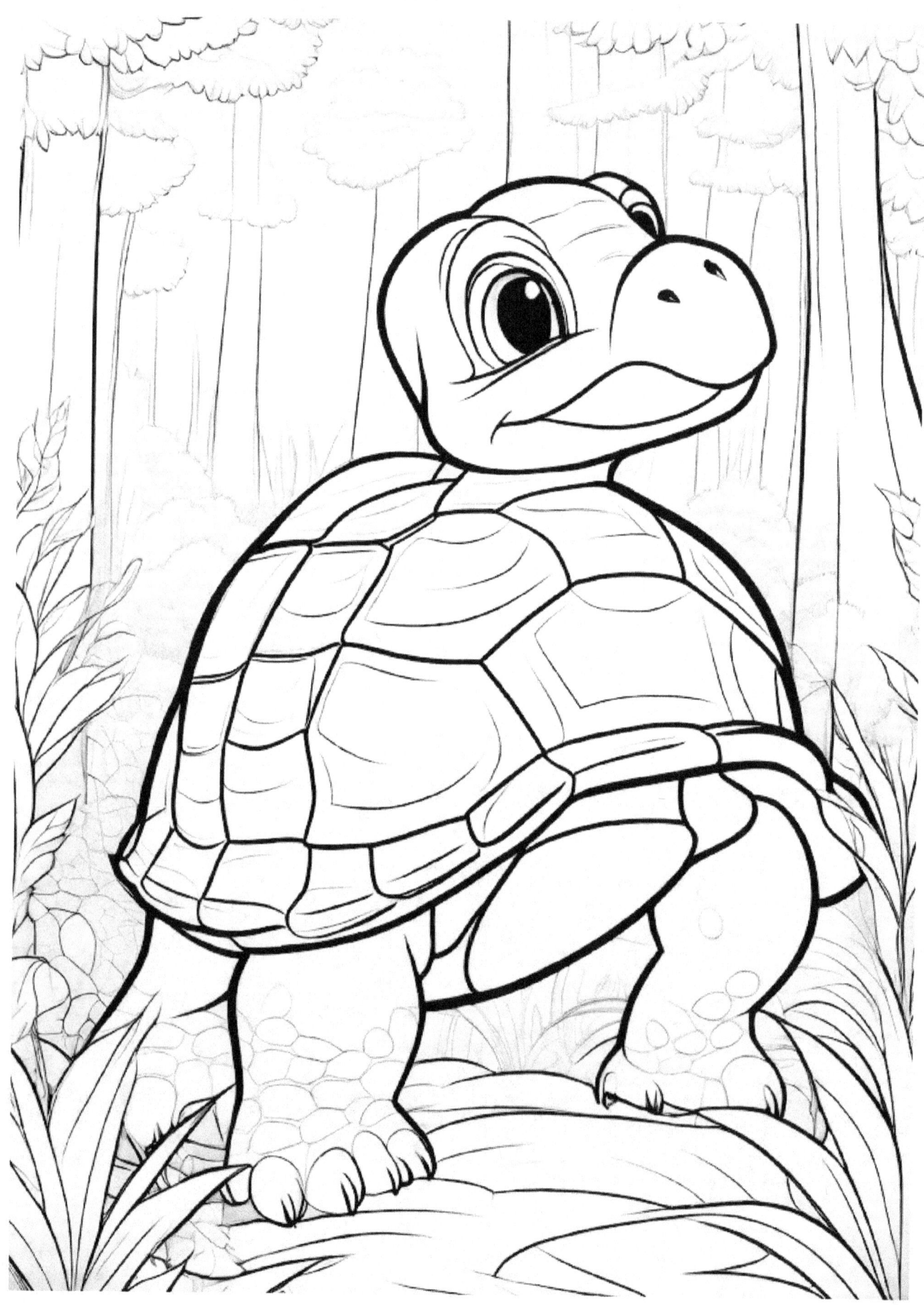

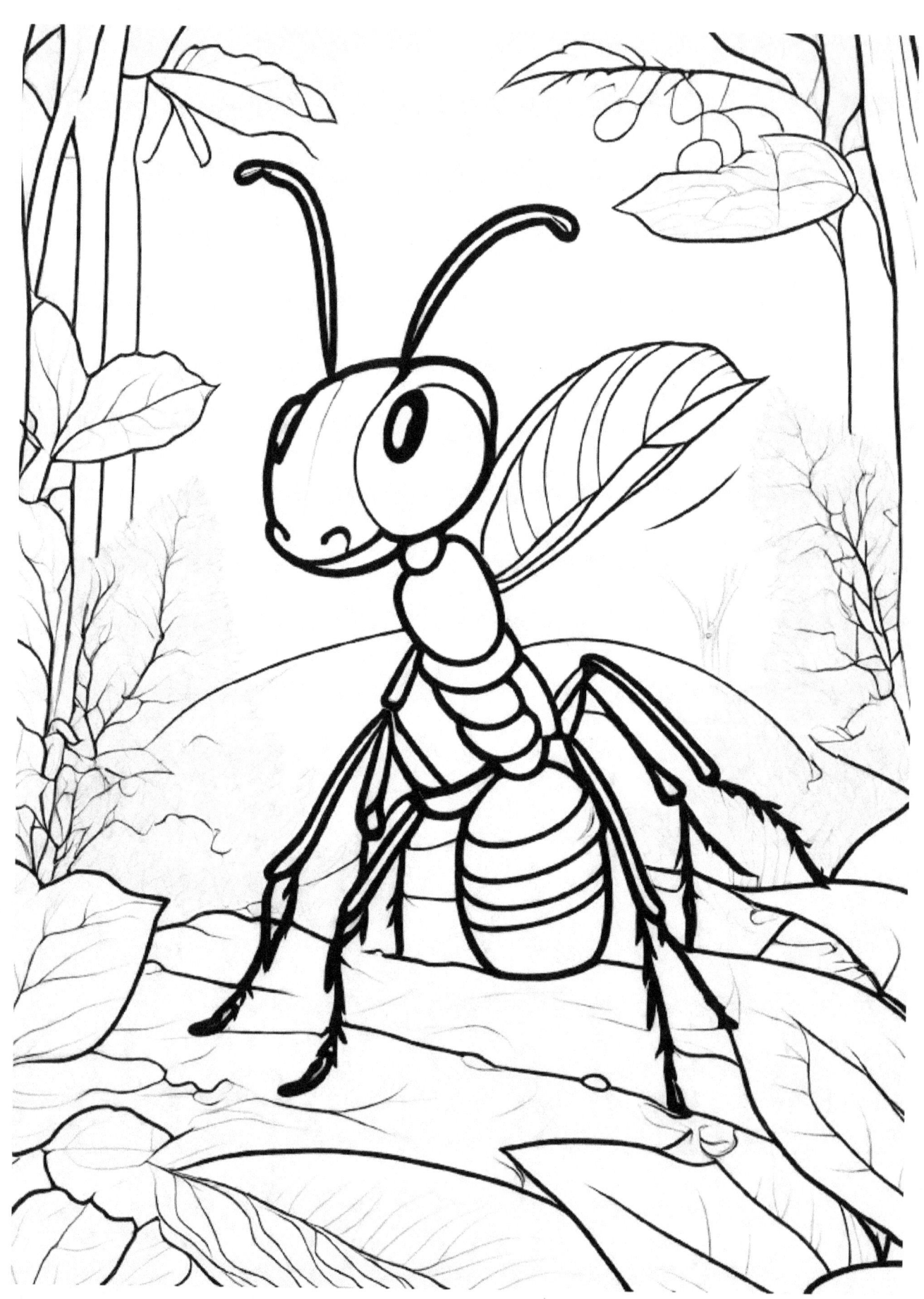

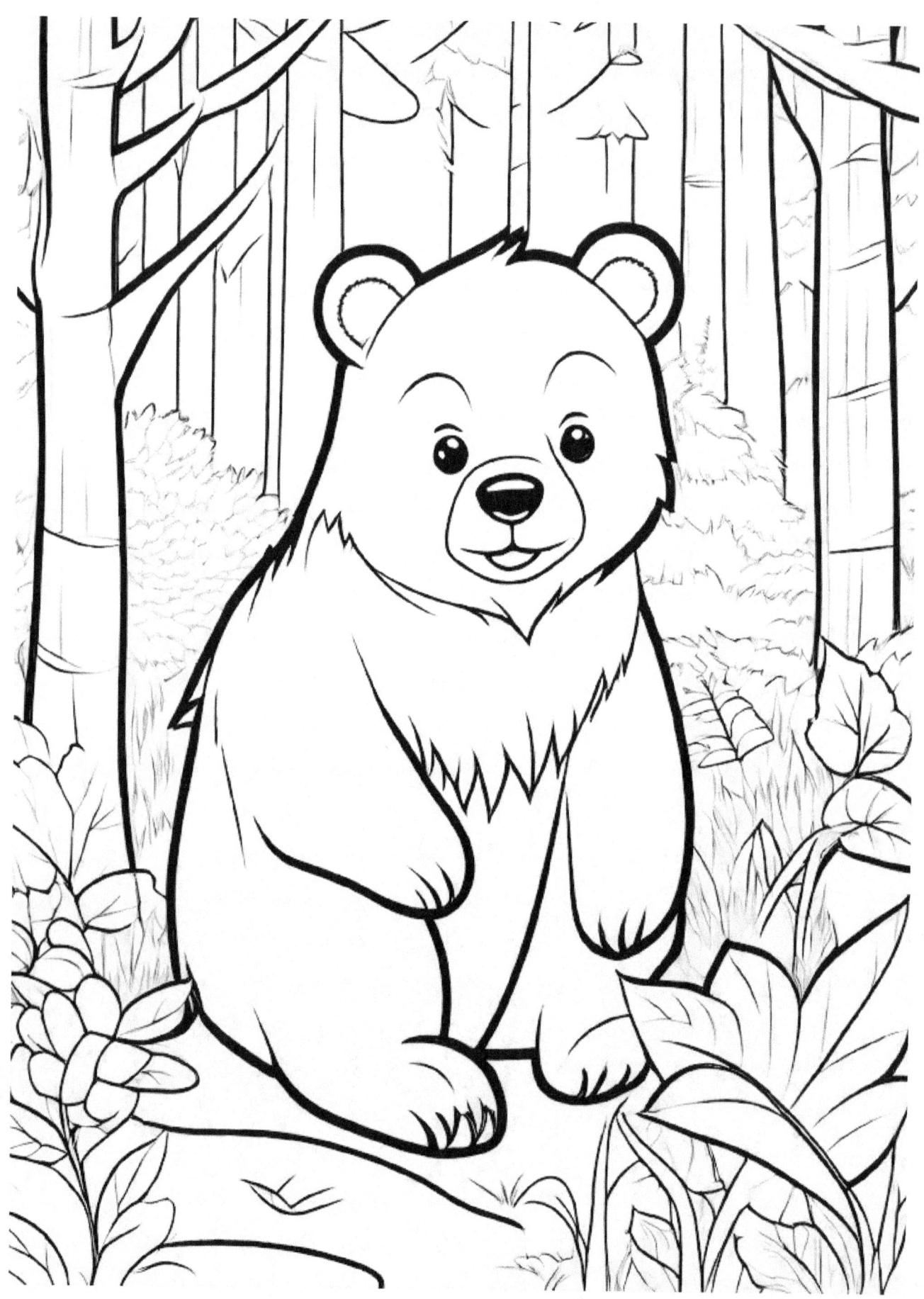

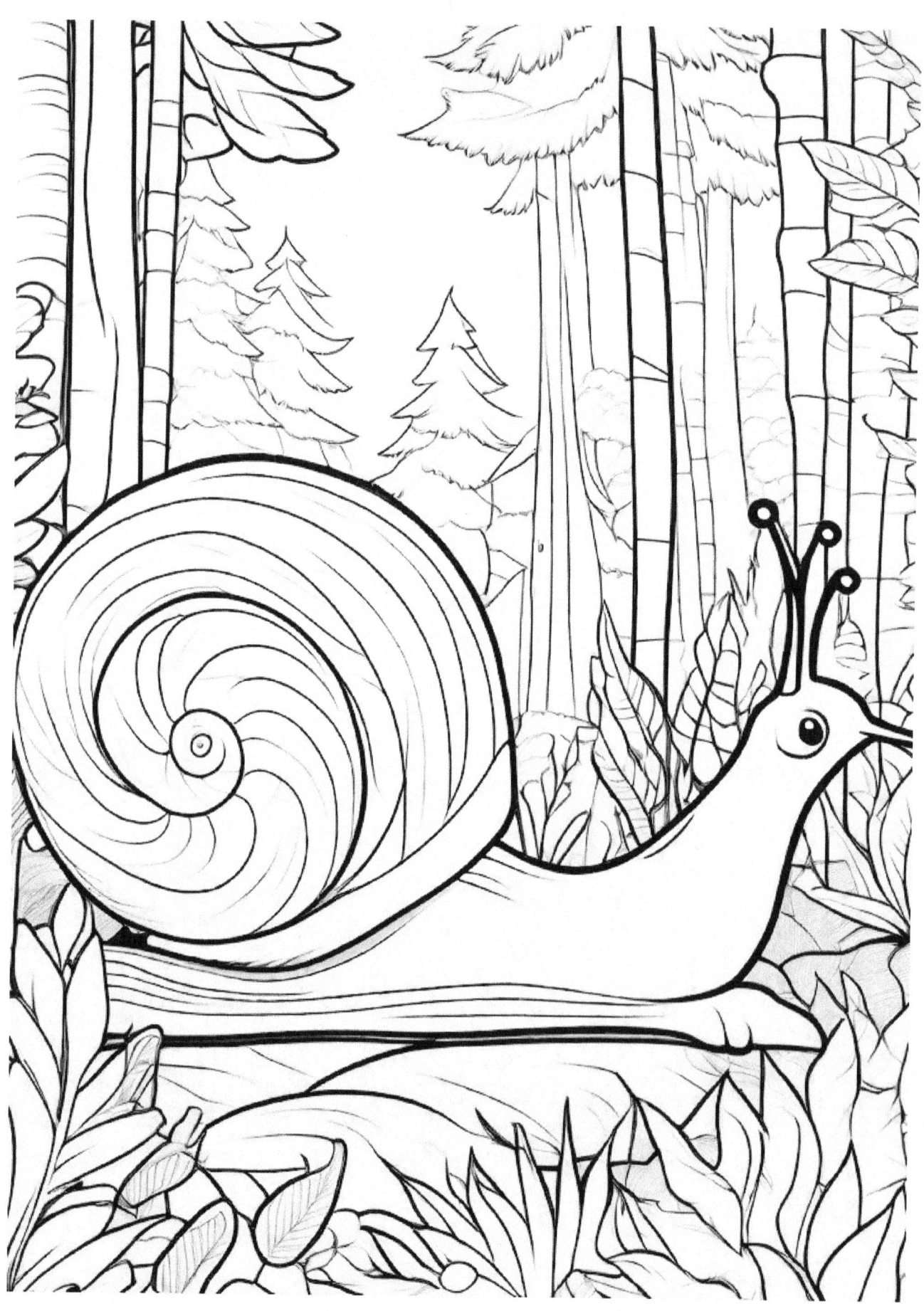